Shattered but Unscathed

Where Science & Philosophy meet 'Spirit'

A psychotherapist's personal journey of grief that unearthed fragmented parts of 'self'

(Integrating Psychology, Neuroscience, Quantum Physics, Existential Philosophy & the Story of Creation)

Rachel Bates

notionpress.com

INDIA • SINGAPORE • MALAYSIA

ISBN 979-8-90510-253-0

Dedication

I would like to dedicate this book to my father, the man who brought me forth into the world, the man who dedicated his life to his wife, his children, his parents, his sisters, their families and to his church.

He fell in love with and married, the most beautiful woman I have ever known in all my life, my mother, and despite the brutal hardships and struggles life threw at them, together, they nurtured and nourished their children and their grandchildren. It appears as if they no longer exist, but through the legacy they left, of their sacrificial love, not only for their children but to all they knew, they will always exist.

To the Creator of my soul and those of all I love, I dedicate myself, my life and all that I could ever be.

Contents

Foreword 7
Reviews 9
Prologue 13
Acknowledgments 15

1. The Tornado 17
2. The Eye of the Storm 23
3. An Anchor 29
4. What Really is Grief? 35
5. Existence & its Dimensions 41
6. Dimensions of Existence vs Dimensions of the Earth 49
7. Spirituality 53
8. What is 'Spirit' 60
9. Soul vs Spirit 71
10. Soul Wounds 77
11. Belief 83
12. Shattered but Unscathed - a Spiritual Perspective 89

Epilogue 97

Foreword

Psychotherapist, Rachel Bates brings us her second book and in doing so, takes a quantum leap from her first searingly personal and deeply moving work.

'Shattered but Unscathed' takes us on another personal, yet highly professional journey through the experience of extreme grief. In the wake of the sudden loss of her father, Rachel likens her experience to finding herself suddenly enveloped and swept up by a tornado.

Her first chapter opens with the statement, "There is a safe spot within every tornado - our job is to find it". And so, the reader is taken on a rare journey of personal analysis, unearthing the inner coping mechanisms of a highly qualified psychotherapist's mind and a well-seasoned, pan-dimensional, healing pathway towards that place of inner peace - the eye of the storm.

The first few chapters look at loss and grief from several metaphorical perspectives, bringing understanding of the various progressive stages that can be expected. Here, through the forms of both testimony and parable, Rachel attempts to help the reader identify with the natural, but non-negotiable process that grief must necessarily follow but offers a glimmer of the light of hope in the process.

From here the book takes a turn into the deep swirling tunnel of the tornado, observing the inner workings of the human body, soul and spirit. Here she draws profound wisdom from the streams of psychology, neuroscience, quantum physics, existential philosophy and faith in a divine creator being. By so doing, she explores human existence in its various dimensions, relating this to the dimensions of planet earth itself and finally, crucially, plunging into the fathomless depths of human spirituality.

This is a superb piece of work on the complex and emotive subject of coping with grief. Despite coming from the mind of an eminently qualified professional psychotherapist, it is entirely accessible to anyone. Its power is intensified by the depth of personal testimony running through its pages. Yet its professional insight gives it an authority and wisdom that comes from a deep well of experience. The cement that holds together all of these diverse threads is the bond of the personal faith of the author in a Being far greater than herself, a faith that is explored, analysed and evaluated as an authentic, living Hope towards the end of the book.

Whether or not you are shattered; whether you feel scathed or unscathed, this personal, professional and enlightening book is well worth your attention!

– Simon Day
Author of *A Tale of 2 CV's*

Review

A soulful and beautiful exploration of human existence, healing, and hope. It flows with poetic grace, offering profound reflections that feel both deeply personal and universally resonant. With remarkable insight, Rachel weaves the physical, psychological, social, and spiritual dimensions of life, creating a narrative that is intimate, thought-provoking, and deeply moving. The writing carries a quiet emotional strength, inviting reflection while offering comfort and clarity.

In a subtle yet significant way, the author reveals scientific and philosophical insight throughout the work, awakening curiosity and gently drawing readers toward deeper spiritual reflection and a yearning to explore the story of creation more deeply. Each page is filled with wisdom, beauty, and compassion, speaking tenderly to the complexities of being human. Rare and memorable, this is a piece of work that not only inspires deep reflection but also leaves a lasting sense of hope, lingering in the heart long after the final page.

– Shravani P Isaac
Manager-Sales & Marketing
Total Environment Homes

Review

'Shattered but Unscathed' is a thoughtful and substantial work that examines grief through the combined lenses of personal experience, professional insight, philosophy, science, and the story of creation. It is not merely a personal account of bereavement, but an attempt to consider grief as an inevitable given of life that can impact the body, mind, soul and spirit.

One of the strengths of this book is the way Rachel draws on her professional background to explore the psychological and emotional impact of loss. Grief is presented not simply as sadness, but as a profound disruption to identity, security, attachment and meaning. This is particularly evident in her reflection on the loss of a parent and the recognition that parental love occupies a unique place in human life.

The book is especially valuable in the way it brings science and philosophy into conversation with spirituality. Psychology and philosophy contribute to our understanding of grief, the framework of human experience, and the existential questions that emerge in times of suffering. Additionally, the narrative of Creation illustrates that hope and the restoration of one's inner being are essential components of human existence.

'Shattered but Unscathed' is therefore a serious reflection on one of life's most painful realities. I would recommend it not only to those who are grieving, but also to those who are questioning, looking for that higher power, searching for truth. Rachel's work encourages the reader to consider that behind the pain of loss there remains the presence of the one who breathed His breath into mankind, and that through the union of the human spirit with that of the spirit of the Creator, there is hope that reaches beyond what science or philosophy can offer.

– Martin Gaunt
Senior Manager-Adult Social Care
West Sussex, UK

Prologue

This book is borne out of my exposure to emotional pain from my years of practice as a mental health practitioner, compounded by my own pain of loss and the journey I needed to navigate, to regain my stability and a sense of being grounded.

My passion is and always has been, to help people understand the importance of mental well-being and shatter the misconceptions of mental illness and dismantle the stigma around it.

Studying the dimensions of human existence as a parallel to the dimensions of the earth on which human life exists has been astounding as it is revelatory of innate wisdom and truth.

Demystifying the concepts of Quantum Physics, Neuroscience, Existential Philosophy & Psychology, and arriving at a point of convergence, has been an exciting journey of how 'consciousness' as the essence of a human being, can contribute to both physical and mental well-being.

Whether you are bereaved and challenged by your journey of grief, or you are a mental health practitioner, facilitating the process of grief, empowering recovery and post-traumatic growth, or someone trying to understand the mysteries of existence, my aim is to help you gain a deeper understanding of how the human body, mind and soul operate as a whole and what it has to offer, in order to find the path to regeneration and restoration of wholesome health.

It is my hope that every reader will discover the unique meaning and purpose of their life through understanding who they really are at the core of their being and the origin of their existence, through the Story of Creation.

Acknowledgments

To my Creator, for inspiring me to inspire whoever would read this book.

To John, my husband, who despite his own storms, stood by me, to weather mine.

To Benjamin, my only child, who stood behind me at a time I thought I was going to lose my balance and walked beside me, as I traversed the journey of my grief.

To my clinical supervisor, the fabulous people I work with, who graciously acknowledged that I too, am prone to the pain of loss and needed time to work through my grief.

To all my beloved cousins, family and friends who showered their love on my parents and have continued to support me through my time of sorrow.

Most importantly, I acknowledge the unconditional love and dedication of my father who instilled in me, the ability to be who I have become today.

1. The Tornado

There is a safe spot within every tornado, our job is to find it

Wait, what's just happened?

Somehow, throughout my whole entire life, the word 'tornado' had never crossed my mind. I had heard about it, read about it but never wondered what the nature and impact of a tornado really was, until today. It is the 4th of November 2025. I am stood in the bustling queue, emotionally numb, waiting to board my home-bound flight back to London, from India and think to myself, "Wait a minute, what's just happened?" I ask myself quietly, am I still standing, still here? Everything felt surreal. I almost feel dissociated and distant from reality.

I know I look calm, like I was just returning from a well-deserved holiday, but only I knew the truth, my world had just shattered. A large part of my world had just collapsed, imploded in on me. I felt as if I was standing in the rubble of what had just come crashing down around me and I wasn't sure where the pieces lay.

This is when the thought of a tornado crossed my mind. It felt like I had just been blown off my feet and swept up by an unexpected tornado, lifted into the air by swirling torrents of loss and an unbearable pain that was ripping my heart apart. I could not explain this, but I seemed to have an inner knowing, deep down in my spirit, that, despite being hurled into the air and violently tossed around, I had landed back, safe on the ground. I felt unharmed but wasn't sure if this was real.

A tornado is a violently rotating column of air that extends from a thunderstorm cloud down to the ground. It can uproot trees, destroy buildings, flip cars and hurl debris at high speeds. They are known to develop and appear suddenly and cause major damage to property and loss of lives. From a scientific view, when warm air on the ground rises quickly into cooler air above, it creates instability in the atmosphere. In the real sense of the word, I found myself in 'a psychological tornado'.

It had become my habit to call my dad every day at about the same time. The 21st of October 2025 was just like any other day when I called, but he did not answer my call. My sister picked up my call. In my spirit, I could sense something was amiss. At this point in time, all I wanted was to just see him, talk to him but I couldn't. I wanted to shout, scream at him, just to ask him to wake up but my sister told me he hadn't responded for a few hours. There were days when he refused to wake up for breakfast, but this was not one of them.

That night, I could not sleep, my spirit was deeply troubled and disturbed. I must have drifted off out of sheer exhaustion when suddenly, I was awoken by my own heart that seemed to be racing. It was one of those strange moments when one knows, and one does not know, a moment of both emotional and cognitive conflict. No matter how hard I tried, I could not sleep nor rest as I could sense a storm coming my way. I could sense it in my entire being. It was like the atmosphere in my inner being unexpectedly turned unstable. I could feel intense anxiety, mental confusion as to what I should be doing, feeling pulled in several directions at once. My mind was swirling, thoughts touching down and then being swept up again, the way a tornado swirls air! The warmth of the love I had for my papa, seemed to have risen quickly out of my heart, into the cold reality of the impending end of his life and it was twisting and turning me on the inside. I wondered if my heart was about to explode. This is it, I thought, I have lost my mother, now I am about to lose my remaining parent and then I will be parent-less, an orphan. Losing parents, at any age, is profoundly disorienting, and can trigger a feeling of being untethered. It felt like the ground underneath was about to give way. I felt as if I needed to prepare myself for the loss of a fundamental part of my identity and purpose of life, all at the same time.

The next morning, I found myself shaking violently in front of my desktop, as I tried to book a ticket to travel to India. I just knew I had to go, to be with my papa, if these were the last hours of his life. My eyes were so blurred from my tears that I could barely see the screen.

I then called my son, Benjamin, (who worked as a flight attendant at the time) to see if he could help me book my ticket. Benjamin was on his aircraft, just about to take off. He did not answer my call, but called back and when he did, all I managed to say was, 'my dad' and then burst into tears. I do not even remember asking him if he would book me a ticket. He said, *mama, let me disconnect the phone, so I can drive home*. He got his captain (the pilot) to let him get off the plane and ran back to his car, to drive home. Within just a couple of hours of calling Benjamin, we were at the airport, checking in. Everything became a blur, I felt as if I was having an out-of-body experience, floating somewhere, and yet I was incredibly grateful that I could leave. Benjamin accompanied me, saying *there's no way I will let you go on your own.*

We arrived in India the next day, and were about forty-five minutes away, on our way from the airport to my sister's house, when we got the one phone call, I have dreaded all my life. My 'papa had breathed his last'. That was it, my father, the man who lovingly raised me and my sister, with no reservations for himself, was now gone. I was desperate to see him, to talk to him one last time, but it wasn't to be. Despite having walked through the grief of losing my mother, I still could not fathom the idea of death as being permanent. The brain refuses to absorb the pain at once. It allows grief to emerge in stages, and I am grateful it does.

I realised that I was now, in the middle of a storm, not a tropical storm but a tornado. It felt like some strange wind had lifted me off the ground on which I stood and it suspended me in the air. At this point in time, I wasn't sure when I would land back on my feet if at all!

Arriving at my sister's house to finally see my father was a strange relief but I was devastated that he wasn't going to open his eyes to see me or talk to me. Just a few weeks prior, he asked me when I was planning to travel to India, and I argued with him that it was not even a couple of months since I had returned from visiting India. He did not argue back but I wish I knew then, what I know now. My papa knew something I did not, but he was not going to tell me.

I would have given anything to have him open his eyes one last time to see me even if he could not talk, just to let him know I was with him. The only comfort I had was to touch his face and feel him still warm. It felt like his heart was still beating, beating to the rhythm of his love for his wife, his children, his grandchildren, his sisters, his nieces, his nephews, for all those he knew and cared about, so tenderly, so generously. Throughout my life, I had poured out my love on my parents, regardless of how far away I was, and I had very little by way of regret and yet, there I stood, wondering if there was anything, just anything else at all, I could have done for him.

The reality of the pain of losing a parent's unconditional love hit me hard when I lost my mother, but I somehow did not expect it to hit again when I lost my father. I naively thought I was prepared for this loss. I knew no one and nothing would replace the love of a parent. The tornado had hit me, threatening to uproot my sense of identity, the meaning and very purpose of my life. This was overwhelming. *The death of any loved parent is an incalculable lasting blow. No one ever loves you again like that. Brenda Uoland*

They say, there is always a place of safety, within the storm, but I was not sure there was one in mine. It felt like a strong wind had literally just uprooted and shredded to pieces, my entire being, turned my world upside down and inside out.

Where was the safe place they call, the 'eye of the storm', in my tornado?

Losing our parents does not mean we have lost the love they poured into us because their love is the seed they sowed, that will bear fruit when watered with joy and gratitude

2. The Eye of the Storm

This storm is you... step right into it, and walk through it, step by step

Scientific research reveals that the eye in a storm is the point of the lowest surface pressure within the entire storm. This is the point around which the centre of the storm rotates. It is the area of 'calm' in the storm. I questioned if this held true in the real storms of life? I needed to find the eye in my storm. I am curious to analyse the characteristics of this kind of storm as a likeness of my psychological tornado, which is unexpected and devastating.

Storms such as hurricanes and tornadoes are studied under the scientific discipline of Meteorology, a branch of the atmospheric sciences. In the very centre of a storm, is the eye of the storm. It is the formation of the eye of the storm that allows weather forecasters and meteorologists to determine that a storm, be it a hurricane or a tornado, is gaining strength. The eye appears clear with few clouds and has lower wind speeds than the rest of the storm. The centre of a tornado is an area of intense, rapidly decreasing pressure, often leading to a small, clear, cylinder of air.

As I went into my room that night, kneeling beside my bed and thanking my Creator for the father and mother He had given me, I felt like, just for a few moments, I could experience the peace in the middle of a storm. Just for a few moments, I had allowed myself to be sucked into the cylinder of the pure air I was breathing. There I was, uncertain of how the future looked, fearful of how I would face life without my parents' enduring love and support, yet at peace, because I knew my parents were 'home' at last. They had reached their destination.

Whilst my tornado was gaining strength, the realisation, that my father was finally free of his earthly responsibilities and from the pain of losing his beloved wife, descended into my spirit. It created that small, clear space wherein I could feel safe to rest. It was here, I regained some of my lost strength. I wasn't ready to dance in the rain ... first I needed to walk through the pain of the loss, but how do I do this? What really did it mean to step into the storm.

When I asked myself that question, I recognised that I was already in the storm but wasn't quite sure, how I could remain in the centre, the place of safety as the noise of the thunderous rain outside was persistent and felt invasive.

It then occurred to me that the few moments of peace I had, kneeling beside my bed that night, was kind of, the centre or the eye of the tornado. But it felt conflicting because I thought, 'well, ok, papa is in a peaceful place but what about me?' 'Am I really at peace?' It felt more like agony and turmoil. But very soon, I realised I need to draw my peace from the truth that he, my papa, was at peace. That gut wrenching anguish was a result of my unwillingness to come to terms with my loss, to submit to the reality of 'death', a reality that felt more like an authority that was heartlessly cruel.

The image below is that of the eye of a storm. It is not difficult to spot the centre, around which the raging sea revolves. It is the calmest part of the storm.

It appears however, that to get to the centre, one must wade through the gusty wind and rough waters, without getting sucked into the fierce power of the current.

I understood now that what I really needed the courage to do was to make a choice. I had to choose, to plunge into the sea of pain, walk through the waves of uncertainty, and anxiety, without allowing myself to be pulled in by the strong currents of hopelessness and despair until I reached the place of 'calm', where I could feel the peace that surpasses understanding. This felt like a whole new dimension, I had read about, talked about, written about, but never experienced first-hand. It was here now. I had to make the choice, and quickly. If I stopped or delayed my decision-making, I could easily get sucked in. I needed to make that choice and there was not much time left to do it.

Many years ago, I was in a very similar situation. I had dropped off mom at her doctor's office for an appointment she had. I then returned home as I had something urgent to attend to. I told mom to wait for me as I would be back to pick her up as soon as I was finished with what I needed to do. When I got out of the house, however, to go and pick up mom, I found the roads flooded. I did hear what felt like a thunderstorm, but did not realise that the roads were flooded, within the space of just a few hours.

I knew I could not use my two-wheeler, which was my mode of transportation at the time, as the water level was too high for me to ride through. So, I decided to walk. I knew this was a risk as I could not see the roads and wasn't sure where the potholes were. I knew my mom would have finished with her consultation. I began to worry that she would be worried as to how I was going to get to her. There were no mobile phones at the time. I slowly made my way to the main road where I found an autorickshaw. The driver was kind enough to let me use his services although he warned me of the danger on the roads.

As I boarded the rickshaw, I told myself, there really is no risk I will not take, to reach my mother and bring her back home. I did not care if I had to walk all the way and got covered by dirty rainwater or if I had to trip and fall over or got soaking wet. There was nothing I was not willing to give up, to bring my mother back to safety.

The autorickshaw did make it to the doctor's office. I ran into the waiting room and found my mom quietly seated. I saw no sign of worry or disturbance in her. A wave of relief washed over me, just to see her waiting for me, calm and quiet. I asked her if she was wondering how I would get there but she said, with total confidence, "I knew you would be here". My mother's faith in me, her child, was child-like. She wasn't oblivious to the weather conditions, but she trusted me to get through it.

My love for her, woven with her trust in me, produced the strength and courage that helped me wade through the storm until I got to where she was. The choice to remain calm was not difficult. 'Love' made the choice, 'trust' helped navigate the path. I found the eye of the storm. Now that I had experienced the 'calm' I was ready to wade through the rough waters again, to get back home.

The storm I found myself in now, however, seemed relentless and overpowering. The love I had for my father, took me to a place of calm but that seemed fleeting since he was not here anymore, to reassure me. I had just lost the only person who loved me without expecting anything in return. So how could I remain in the 'calm'. I could not sustain that moment.

In some ways, the love I had for my papa, seemed to exacerbate the pain of losing him, and this was compounded by the loss of my beloved mother. Does love hurt so bad? Does loving one mean risking the pain of losing them? Perhaps, grief is the price we pay for love.

If the storm is me and all I needed to do was to step into the storm, then I realised, I just had to step inside of me, in other words, find my inner strength and ground myself in the faith and hope I have.

As I felt tossed by the wind of the storm, I realised, what I really needed now, was an anchor. Perhaps my anchor would be my hope, my faith. Faith? I believed in faith, but on what should I cast my faith. I believed in trust, but in whom or what do I put my trust? People often ask the question, do you have faith in yourself, do you trust yourself? I do believe in myself and have faith in who I am, but how could I count on the faith I thought I had in myself, when I had been reduced to what feels like crumbled clay or shattered glass?

When we discover how love and trust can produce calm and peace, we have found the eye in any storm

3. An Anchor

An anchor is meant to hold you steady, not drag you down with it
Hope anchors the soul

An anchor is the heavy metal device attached to a boat or ship by a cable that is dropped into the water to grab the seabed to keep the vessel from drifting due to wind or a current and hold it in place.

The Nautical Institute in 'the science of anchoring' states that *anchors are designed for harbours and sheltered areas. If the vessel is likely to yaw or pitch, then the mariner must be alert to the possibility of dragging. Anchoring equipment is intended for temporary mooring of a ship within a harbour or sheltered area. The equipment is not designed to hold a ship off fully exposed coasts in rough weather or to stop a ship when it is moving or drifting.*

Now, this is exactly how it felt. The love of my parents that kept me anchored could not weather the storm of their loss as my ship seemed to be drifting, moving into unchartered waters. It felt like my love for them was dragging me down as I was being swept by the waves of the sudden realisation that, no one will ever love me like they did. No one will be as proud of me, as they were.

No one would believe in me, the way my parents did. My sense of self, I thought, was anchored in my parents' belief and faith in me.

An anchor symbolises meaning, a goal, a direction that offers hope and strength, with the aim to always stay grounded. After I lost my mother, I continued to stay grounded as my dad gave me the purpose and direction to keep sailing. But losing my father seemed to dislodge my anchor, my stability, my meaning, my hope and strength. I was no longer sailing as my coast was unexpectedly exposed to rough weather, just drifting aimlessly. I became alert to the possibility of my anchor dragging me, not grounding me as it did before.

Just two days after we arrived in India, we were preparing to bury my dad. I knew I had to bid my final farewell. It all felt surreal. When I woke up that morning, I was cruelly reminded that I was going to have to see my father for the very last time and then, I will no longer have my parents left on the earth.

As I walked into the church for the funeral service, there was this wishful thinking, I need to find my papa so I could sit next to him. I knew he would be looking for me. I knew most of the people that had arrived there, from about three decades ago. Although it felt comforting to see them, the people who knew my parents for many years, I did not know how I was going to transit from expecting my papa to smile to seeing him lying in a casket, cold and lifeless. What a heartless severance?

Who ever invented death? I wonder if this is the role of grief, the journey from being faced with the shock of the loss of life to the point of accepting the loss of life?

To my dismay, I saw my papa entering the church, only this time, he was being transported, surrounded by gentle hands and solemn faces. The sight was devastating and felt surreal, making the reality of his absence painfully clear. My heart ached as I realised this would be the last time I would see him.

He was not going to see me or smile and say to me 'I knew you'd be here'. When that reality struck me, try as I might, I was no longer grounded. I was afloat, drifting. My anchor seemed to drag me away from my harbour. I did not feel sheltered anymore. I am not sure if I appeared to be strong and resilient on the outside. But on the inside, I felt torn apart like a piece of rag. At this time, I did not feel I could be put together again, ever. I felt like a fragile clay pot that fell over and broke into a million pieces.

At the burial place, I was comforted by the many friends and family, who had taken the time and made the effort to stand beside us. But as I turned and walked away, knowing that I would never ever see my papa again, there was this sense of peace and at the same time, anxiety and emptiness. My emotions were conflicting. I remind myself that I have just been traumatised by the loss of my dad and it is normal to feel pulled between intense opposing feelings, of both anxiety and hope.

For the rest of that day, I was surrounded by a loving family and gracious friends. As I got into bed that night, I knew that despite the pain and what felt like a loss of purpose, I was in a state of 'calm', not out of the relief that papa was no longer suffering but because he had left us a lifetime of love, enough to carry on life after him. Neither my mother nor my father took back with them, their love for me, their belief and faith in me; they left it all behind and now it is mine to treasure. According to Huganir, director of the Johns Hopkins Department of Neuroscience, our brain treasures loving memories through a process called 'synaptic plasticity' wherein brain cells grow stronger every time we recall a fond memory.

The next few days I was in India, felt like a roller coaster ride as there were days of happiness, as I recalled childhood memories with my sister but there were other painful days when memories brought back joy but along with it, deep sorrow, as my yearning for my parents increased. I did not know where to place my pain. Should I bury it deep inside so no one could see it, or should I let it surface so I could walk through it? I chose to let it surface but it felt like walking through an ocean. If grief is an ocean, I can sense, it is my responsibility to just stay afloat until I found my anchor, amid the danger and risk of being swept away by the flood of pain.

I remember, as a child, I loved going to the beach with my parents and my little sister. As soon as we got in and found a place to sit, on the sand, mom would let me take off my shoes and go with my dad, to dip my toes into the water. My dad always made sure, my hand was in his as I slowly edged closer to the water. On one occasion, I caught myself squealing with delight as I was being pulled into the deep as the sand under my feet began to shift. It seems that I was oblivious to the fact that if I did not stop myself, I could soon be dragged away into the deep. I noticed my feet were no longer firm and steady. They were shifting! I was quickly being carried into the water. Just then, my dad pulled me back rather abruptly, back onto the sand. This is when he told me that whenever I am stood on the edge of the water on a beach, I need to dig my feet as deep as I could, into the wet sand. This he said, would ground me and I will not be easily carried away by the huge waves that come crashing onto the sand. I then learned that it was not dangerous to play with the waves, so long as I kept digging my feet deeply into the sand. The sand will feel slippery when the waves relentlessly beat onto the shore, but I need to press in persistently, so, my feet are firmly embedded in the ground. I did not realise at the time, that digging my feet deep into the ground had to be a conscious intentional act.

This, I know now, is what I needed to do, persistently dig my feet deeper into the soil of belief, faith and trust, as the waves of the pain of my loss relentlessly threatened to swamp me, washing away the ground under my feet.

As the mariner of my boat, I felt I was being dragged away by this but then, as I reflected on it, I became conscious that they may have departed now, but the secure attachment I had, as a consequence of their unconditional love for me, their faith, their belief, in me, is all I need to produce in me, that sense of internal calm and stability. This, as I see it now, has anchored me and made me into the person I have become.

I remember the days when I waited outside my school, my college, and then my different workplaces, for my papa who faithfully dropped me off and picked me up. He did this every day of my growing up life. He never once put his own needs before ours, be it my mother's, my sister's or mine.

As I dig my feet deeper, I realise that, on the one hand, grief makes me feel loyal to my parents but on the other it constantly reminds me of what I no longer have, and this did not feel like a positive thinking process, nor did it leave me feeling rewarded. I know, however, that I must grieve, for 'grieving' is the only way to resolve grief. But then, can grief be resolved?

Faith cannot make the waves disappear but will give you the resilience to stand, until the storm passes

4. What Really is Grief?

While grief is a tidal force, the pain of loss can feel like a flood that will drown you.

Why is grief such a big deal? People say, 'Oh he is grieving' or, 'Have you grieved?' Am I grieving if I feel extremely sad? Is grief associated to losing someone you love? Does grief lead to depression?

The American Psychological Association defines 'grief' as the anguish experienced after a significant loss, affecting individuals emotionally, physically, and socially; and 'depression' as a negative affective state, ranging from unhappiness and discontent to an extreme feeling of sadness, pessimism, and despondency, that interferes with daily life. This can include various physical, cognitive, and social changes such as altered eating or sleeping habits, lack of energy or motivation, difficulty concentrating or making decisions and withdrawal from social activities.

Grief therefore can be associated with the pain of any significant loss, not necessarily the death of a loved one. However, grief is not depression. When grief is not addressed at all, it can lead to depression and/or anxiety or anger and sometimes a combination of them all.

In my work as a psychotherapist, I have often encountered people looking for help with anger management and found unattended grief lurking beneath their anger.

The only way to process grief, is to grieve, in other words, to experience the pain, wade through the deep rough waters. This means that grieving is a natural, healthy response to loss and therefore, not a symptom of depression. We often tend to think that, experiencing emotional pain would leave us feeling vulnerable and weak and so we try to bury the anguish of our loss. Denying emotional pain for fear of feeling susceptible to vulnerability can cause one to conceal it and this is what can eventually lead to depression. Dr. Edith Egar states: *It is not what comes out of us, but what remains inside of us, that makes us sick. You cannot heal what you do not feel.* Dr Egar, reiterates, *the opposite of depression is expression.*

This clarifies that talking about the one we lost or expressing our shock and narrating the story of our loss and pain, helps process our grief. One of the common ways in which people react to grief is to bury themselves in their daily routine, or more specifically, find new projects to work on as it gives them something else to engage with. This is not necessarily an incorrect way to deal with grief, provided they make the time and space to allow the pain of the loss, to surface. Embracing the pain of loss empowers one to re-engage with life and re-engaging with life, does not mean forgetting and moving on. It means regaining structure and control in daily life, restoring a sense of personal agency and purpose.

When grief is not attended to, it fills the heart with emptiness. This is the time, emptiness feels heavy. Emotional distress causes the body to release stress hormones like cortisol and adrenalin which in turn produces a sensation of tightness or heaviness. This is what makes the heart feel heavy.

A young man I worked with once, told me he did not understand why he unexpectedly reached a point in his life when he realised, he could not go on any further, as he just did not feel like himself and this confused him. As a father of two very young children he could not, not carry on with his life and responsibilities. He had had a mental breakdown, and it terrified him. During the course of therapy, he talked about the loss of his father, claiming that he had overcome his grief since he had managed to get back to work within a couple of weeks. It transpired however, that he had carefully buried his grief, so he did not have to feel the pain. If he did not feel his pain, he did not have to confront it, nor deal with it. As he unearthed his grief, he was challenged by having to allow his pain to surface, but doing this gradually helped him re-engage with his sense of personal agency, his purpose.

Now that I was confronted by my own grief, I knew I had no alternate routes in my journey of grief. I needed to take the time and make the space to grieve, to allow my sadness to surface, so I could confront it. When we are faced with emotional pain that is incomprehensible, it is easier to avoid talking about it as it is uncomfortable, and we fear it would evoke more pain. From my own experience of working with bereavement, I know that expressing emotional pain can feel worse at first, but it ultimately helps release its harmful effects. *Suffering is caused, not by the pain itself, but by our resistance to it. Accepting that some things are beyond our control, would mean we are in the flow of life, not fighting against the current. Author unknown.*

In other words, exposing pain, weakens its strength. Inhibiting emotional pain on the other hand, can empower it to produce chronic stress responses, causing the body to remain in a heightened state of alertness, potentially producing cardiovascular issues, immune system suppression through constant release of cortisol from stress, chronic pain and illness, hormonal imbalances and the like. It can also produce mental and emotional consequences such as anxiety, depression, emotional numbness, increased shame and guilt, social disconnection and addictive behaviours.

Karolyn Gazella, in his book, 'The Harmful Effects of Unresolved Grief' states that 84% of people who experience loss report that it negatively affects their daily lives, either physically, emotionally or both. He goes on to say that grief is an emotional experience that touches every dimension of life. It shows up in the body, overwhelms cognition, impacts relationships and potentially fractures the spirit.

I recall talking about the loss of my dad with a friend who asked me how old he was. When I told her his age, she immediately told me, *Oh, his end came at a good age,* and I found myself agreeing with her and then it seemed the subject of conversation quickly changed. It felt as if she was telling me I did not need to be upset and sad since he had lived long enough and was old enough to die. Perhaps she was not conscious of her insensitivity to my state of grief, but it was almost as if I was not permitted to allow my grief to surface in her presence and so I did not. This however, made me uninterested in carrying on my conversation with her. No one should have to need permission to grieve because loss is inevitable and everyone has a right to grieve; everyone needs to grieve their loss. While it is important to make the time and space to grieve, it is essential, to allow for the emotional pain of others around us, to be expressed, so they know they can grieve, because grieving is a healthy response to loss. More importantly, loss of parents is not preventable and grief of losing parents is not defined by their age.

When we lose a parent or a child or close relative or even a close friend, the disorientation we can feel, even if only temporarily, is one of losing part of ourselves. My parents were integral parts of me, my life, my identity, my purpose, my meaning in life, my very existence. Does this mean that some pieces of my sense of identity could break away and my soul could feel fragmented? My life is meaningful and fulfilling but it seems that there are some parts on the inside that feel empty. How do I reconcile with that partial emptiness of my existence? Does emptiness mean 'nothingness'?

But first 'What is existence'?

'Grieving' or processing grief does not obliterate or resolve the pain of the loss. It helps re-integrate the fragmented parts of self

5. Existence & its Dimensions

The purpose of existence is to bring light to the darkness of being

Those of us who are alive are aware that we exist. If we have lost a loved one, we believe that they existed and because they are no longer alive, we say that they no longer exist. What then is the need to understand 'existence' as a concept?

To exist is to have a 'being', to be present, simply put, to be alive. However, 'existence' is a phenomenal concept as it is studied through the experience of consciousness. The word 'exist' originates from the Latin word 'existere' which meant 'to emerge', to 'come forth', to 'be visible', to 'stand firm'. It is the 'emergence' as opposed to remaining 'dormant' that brings light. Human beings are not 'dark' in themselves, but often just fail to see the light inside them that needs to be brought forth.

Ancient Greek philosophers like Plato and Aristotle laid the foundations for the understanding of the concept of existence being the essence of objects and consciousness. Plato distinguished between the physical and the spiritual realm, considering the latter as the more authentic realm. Aristotle on the other hand, focused on the concrete and material aspects of existence, emphasising the importance of gathering information through sight, sound, touch, taste and smell, as these are measurable, observable data.

Quantum physics, which is the study of the interaction between matter and energy, explains 'existence' by proposing that reality is not built by solid building blocks but rather from probabilistic fields of energy that only take definite form through interaction.

'Existentialism', a philosophical movement that emphasises on individual existence, freedom, and choice, posits that individuals are free and responsible agents determining their own development through the acts of their human will. In 1958, Rollo May introduced the framework of the four worlds of existence and in 1984, Emmy van Deurzen, used this framework, to create a practical map for psychotherapy: the physical environment, the social world, the inner world of self, and the transcendent or spiritual world; the core framework of the human being: the body, mind, heart and soul.

At the physical dimension, individuals relate to their environment and to the givens of the natural world around them. At the social dimension, individuals relate to others as they interact with the world around them. At the psychological dimension, individuals relate to their inner selves and in this way create a personal world. This dimension includes views about their own character, their experience, and their future possibilities, the paradoxical strengths and weaknesses. People search for a sense of identity, a feeling of being substantial and having a sense of self.

At the spiritual dimension individuals are said to have a need to connect with a higher self, to relate, to create a sense of an ideal world, an ideology, and a philosophical outlook. It is here that they find meaning by putting all the pieces of the puzzle together for themselves. People create their values in search of something that matters enough to live or die for, something that has ultimate or eternal validity. *There is divine meaning in the life of the world of man, of human persons, of you and me. Buber 2004:66.* Dr. Cassar, 2012, referring to Buber, writes: *for Buber, meaning is something that we discover, not invent, and the only way to find our meaning is through our relationship with God. You need God, the higher power, to 'be'.*

This demonstrates that it is the function of the spiritual dimension that enables discovery of self; the ability to perceive self; interact with the environment; comprehend one's world view and the very purpose of existence.

The loss of my parents however, produced a possibility of nothingness as an indispensable counterpart of my quest for the eternal, and urges me explore further, my question, 'does emptiness mean nothingness?' Emptiness usually means a lack of something, like an empty room or emotionally speaking, a sense of void. However there still is a space, a structure or even a person, just that there is content missing. It could mean a lack of essence. In physics, empty space refers to a region that contains fields and fluctuations; it is not considered absolute nothingness. 'Nothingness' generally suggests a complete absence of anything, no objects, no space, no time, no properties. However, in western philosophy, thinkers like Martin Heidegger and Jean-Paul Satre believed that nothingness, as tied to human consciousness could be the gaps, absences or negations that allow us to think and choose. This illuminates the fact that emptiness does not mean nothingness, neither does nothingness mean emptiness. In effect it could mean the availability of space for creativity or discovery of the existent essence, the unique potential in every human being. It is this existent essence, the unique potential, that really is the light, inside every individual.

Therefore, the pain of loss can be understood as the consciousness of an absence that allows us the space to think, to make new choices, to explore, to re-discover. This consciousness to think, to choose, is what lies, not in the physical or social or even the psychological dimension of 'self', but at the very core of one's existence, the 'spiritual' dimension.

It would, therefore, be useful to explore 'existence' and the impact, processing grief bears on existence, from a physical, social, psychological & spiritual perspective:

From a *physical* perspective, existence is defined as the state of having a presence within a continuum, characterized by the interactions between matter and energy. Modern physics interprets existence through quantum mechanics where vacuum is not emptiness, but a fluctuating field of virtual particles that pop in and out of existence.

Thus, the emptiness I experience on losing my parents, is just a fluctuating field of short-lived imperceptible particles, the acute emotional pain that appears and then seems to become annihilated almost instantly, to conserve energy and momentum, creating a restless ocean of energy. This is called vacuum energy. Vacuum is therefore, not 'nothing'. It is foundational non-zero energy that acts as a physical background in the world of our reality.

The initial shock of the death of a loved one pops into existence but addressing this pain, can soften the blow of the loss, instilling a desire to derive new meaning. It also helps create and conserve the energy that can contribute to one's growth and purpose in life. An unwillingness to address the pain of grief, on the other hand can leave one mentally drained with little energy because the grief has been pushed down in the hope that it can be buried. Buried pain however festers, silently releasing stress hormones and prolonged stress drains mental energy, affecting both physical and mental well-being.

From a *social* perspective, existence is defined as the patterned, meaningful life constructed around achieving shared cultural milestones, such as education, career, and family, within specific time constraints. It is a negotiated 'theory of social behaviour' rather than just biological life, where personal identity is a mix of agency and societal expectations.

When grief is shared and comfort received through the compassion of family or community, it can construct shared cultural values and reinforce the sense of belonging and acceptance, strengthening one's resilience, creating new energy to grow and mature, rather than stagnate with a minimal motivation to survive.

From a *psychological* perspective, existence as understood through existential psychology, focuses on the lived experience of being a human in the world, rather than seeing behaviour as purely mechanistic or predetermined. It emphasises that individuals are in a constant process of 'becoming' or 'self-creating', deriving meaning from their life experiences rather than inheriting it. This can be accomplished only through introspection and self-awareness.

When the loss of a loved one is accepted as a lived experience, and grief, processed, it helps contribute towards the 'becoming' of self. A mental perception of loss as part of life's continuum helps achieve the energy that will act as the source of strength, not just to survive the loss, but to move forward with purpose.

From a *spiritual* perspective, existence is the unfolding journey of consciousness or of the soul, where physical life is a temporary experience rather than the totality of being. It is generally viewed as an eternal reality where the material world is a lower dimension or a 'school' for spiritual evolution.

Existential *philosophy* lends the understanding that spiritual existence involves realising a profound connection to a higher power. Spirituality often entails a relationship with a reality that exists outside the five senses, involving a deeper intuitive understanding of the soul. Humanity is understood as the human spirit manifesting physically, to learn, grow, and experience, with the physical body acting as an embodiment of the eternal self.

This is endorsed by Dr. Van Deurzen, a world-renowned clinical psychologist & philosopher, referenced earlier in this chapter:

When people rediscover their inner connectedness to something greater than themselves, to some ideal which will lift them beyond their everyday struggles, a new motivation flows inside of them, which can carry them through difficulties with unerring purposefulness.

Thus, the spiritual dimension, at the very core, provides the structural integrity of existence at large, the fundamental elements of which are: Individuality: the sense of self with the need to become; Morality & Ethics: the innate biological predisposition for empathy, fairness, moral values; Connectivity: the need to relate, to connect with something greater than self; Consciousness: not just perception and cognition, but an underlying sense of inner awareness, a deep sense of knowing; Meaning & Purpose: the essence of learning, growing and becoming, to achieve a sense of fulfilment.

It is my consciousness, the inner awareness at this spiritual dimension that helps me understand how I have anchored my boat at a time I felt I was being tossed around by the storm of my loss. Although I felt uprooted and destabilised from a physical, social and psychological perspective, it was my conscious relatedness, at the spiritual dimension, with that higher power, that propels me to make sense of my loss, find meaning, to learn, to grow and become, that kept me and continues to keep me grounded.

While I am aware that there would be no human existence without the existence of the earth, I am intrigued as to how the dimensions of human existence on earth are parallel to the dimensions of the earth itself.

The physical and mental well-being of human existence is dependent on the interaction between the physical, emotional, mental and spiritual dimensions. A disturbance in any one dimension can disrupt the entire network.

6. Dimensions of Existence vs Dimensions of the Earth

Earth's dimensions, reflect the indigenous wisdom of divine artistry of the Universe

The divine artistry of the totality of all space, time, matter and energy encompassing billions of galaxies in celestial alignment, a manifestation of a divine blueprint, has got to indisputably be created by indigenous wisdom, higher than the Universe itself. This magnificent universe existed long before quantum physics could explain it.

One such divine masterpiece of creation is the way in which the dimensions of human existence reflects the dimensions of the existence of the earth.

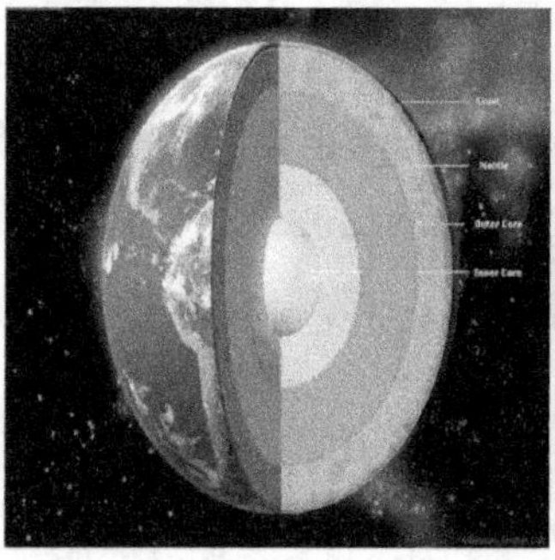

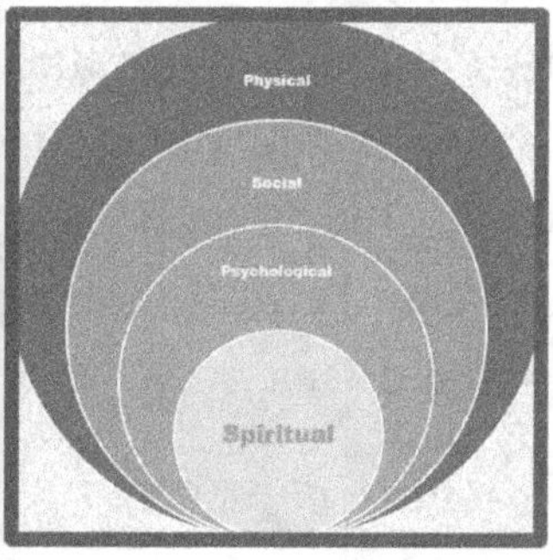

The *crust* is the outermost structure of the earth that functions as the solid protective outer skin of the planet providing a stable habitat for life, just as the outer dimension of physicality in the human existence serves as a structured tangible framework designed to organise and experience reality.

The *mantle* of the earth is the layer that acts as an insulating blanket between the core and the crust, regulating the thermal environment. Relatedly, the social dimension of human existence acts as a bridge between an individual's internal experience and their connection with others in the external world, through shared meanings, responsibilities and interactions. The secure attachments with parents or caregivers and meaningful relationships with others, can help influence emotional regulation and self-actualisation. Secure individuals remain relatively undisturbed during stressful times, can recover faster from episodes of distress, contributing to their overall emotional and mental well-being. The secure attachment acts as the insulating blanket that protects one from the effects of stress.

The *outer core* of the earth is the liquid layer of iron and nickel that creates and generates a magnetic shield that protects the planet from harmful solar radiation. Likewise, the psychological dimension, by utilising cognitive and emotional faculties, acts as a buffer against existential crises.

The *inner most core* of the earth plays a crucial role in creating the magnetic field that protects the earth.

It provides insight into the evolution of the planet. Without the inner core and its magnetic field, the earth might lose its atmosphere and become a barren planet. Identically, the spiritual dimension, at the inner core of human existence, underlies physical reality and bridges the gap between mind and matter. The soul is viewed as a living, intelligent quantum-like field that carries emotional information such as love, joy, peace and gratitude which influences the body's physical bio-electrical fields. The body's bio-electrical field is the complex network of electrical currents and surrounding electromagnetic fields, generated by living cells, tissues, and organs. Without the spiritual dimension, the magnetic field, human existence will lose its atmosphere of consciousness, making life bereft of meaning and purpose.

Researchers have discovered that the core of the earth, the geological centre of the planet primarily consists of solid iron and nickel, containing significant carbon, oxygen and silicon which influences its solidification and density. This is consistent with the core of human existence, the 'soul' that encompasses wisdom, compassion, intuition, the sense of belonging, connectivity, consciousness, meaning and purpose, the moral compass, the very source of life and energy. It appears to awaken within oneself, the consciousness that this physical life is a temporary experience in the light of something far superior, and that in reality, life, although in natural existence, is spiritual. It is this consciousness of connectivity, the source of energy at the spiritual dimension that solidifies the essence of life, through the meaning and purpose it generates.

Exploring 'spirituality', therefore, could help identify its role in the well-being of human beings.

The Universe is not purely materialistic, but rather an intricate web of energy and consciousness, which explains why human existence, cannot survive without the intricate connection between consciousness and energy

7. Spirituality

Spirituality is the diamond mine inside of you

It seems that being 'spiritual' is not a modern-time state of being and the reason for this could potentially lie in the assumption that one needs to be religious to be spiritual.

The word 'spirituality' usually seems to associate itself with 'religion' and religion, as a fixed doctrine is no longer relevant. According to the National Health Service, *'spirituality' is a universal, personal and non-religious-exclusive human experience focused on finding meaning, purpose and hope, particularly during illness or loss. It encompasses how individuals experience connection to themselves, others, nature and the transcendent, with an aim to support holistic wellbeing beyond physical care.*

Powell (2001) writes "Sigmund Freud, 1927, saw religion as a massive defence against neurosis and Carl Jung, 1959 defined the soul, as the living thing in man". He states that *psychiatry has paid little attention to spirituality* and yet a survey carried out by the Mental Health Foundation in 1997, showed that over 50% of service users hold religious or spiritual beliefs they see as important in helping them cope with mental illness.

The more recent 2024-25 survey found that 67% of adults say spirituality or religion is important for mental well-being.

The word 'spiritual' generally refers to a belief in the context of seeking meaning through a connection to something greater than self, that would offer inner peace. The word 'spirit' as part of the word 'spirit-uality' refers to the human spirit. The human spirit can be understood as the life force or energy within, that is produced by its connection to the beyond. This would signify that, the human spirit is an inherent part of every human being, regardless of our understanding or belief of it.

Max Planck, the father of Quantum Physics, who won the Nobel Prize in 1918, for the services he rendered to the advancement of physics by his discovery of energy quanta, writes: *Both religion and science require a belief in God. For believers, God is in the beginning, and for physicists, He is at the end of all considerations. To the former He is the foundation, to the latter, the crown of the edifice of every generalised world view.*

Quantum physics explains spiritual dimension through a concept that suggests, reality is not merely physical, but deeply interconnected and non-material at its core. The concept of a non-material interconnection suggests a pre-existence of the elements that connect.

Ancient Greek philosophy claims spirituality to be the alignment with one's soul, which is immortal, belonging to a non-physical realm. Existential philosophers approached spirituality as a discovery of one's authentic self and the meaning of existence. Metaphysics explains spirituality as an expression of one's spirit, through participation in their consciousness. The secular view of spirituality focuses on personal awareness, mindfulness and connection.

Viktor Frankl, an Austrian neurologist, psychiatrist, philosopher and holocaust survivor (1905-1997) posits that *spirituality is part of every human being because it is what makes man, human. However, this dimension often lies in the unconscious and needs to be brought into conscious awareness, in order that man could reach his full potential and create meaning*. 'Spirituality' according to him is the uniquely human 'noetic' (translated in Greek as 'spirit') dimension, distinct from psychological/ biological factors, oriented towards finding meaning, freedom and responsibility. He emphasised that it is the indestructible conscious core of the human being, which has the capacity to overcome physical suffering or mental turmoil.

For Frankl, 'consciousness' as part of spirituality, is often found in the 'unconscious'. When the traumatic events in life disrupt the normal psychological functioning of human existence, consciousness can be pushed down into the unconscious. Neuroscientific research, indicates that spiritual practices such as prayer, worship and meditation can structurally and functionally alter the brain, impacting the physiological, neurological, and psychological well-being, as follows:

It can enhance executive function and emotional regulation; alter neurotransmitter levels (the body's chemical messengers) in the central nervous system that acts as the brain's calming agent, alleviating anxiety, stress and fear while promoting sleep and relaxation; increase dopamine, the hormone that is responsible for feelings of pleasure, motivation and reward; increase serotonin, the crucial hormone that plays a key role in functions such as mood, sleep, digestion, wound healing, bone health, blood clotting and sexual desire; increase production of oxytocin, the hormone that manages female and male reproductive systems, including labour, delivery and lactation, promoting positive emotions such as love, bonding, compassion, peace, gratitude and hope, thereby reducing anxiety and depression. In effect, spirituality enhances emotional connection, consciousness, mindful compassion, purposeful choices, and diminishes anxiety, depression, and cognitive decline.

The global Journal of Medical Research in the context of spirituality, describes all things as energy, with the human body having a nonlinear electromagnetic field, or 'aura'.

Just as strumming a guitar produces vibrations that create sound waves, a nervous system that is overstimulated or stressed causes internal vibrations, which can potentially manifest as an emotional dysregulation, through neurotransmitters that are responsible for generating, controlling, and spreading the electrical signals that form the basis of the body's bio-electromagnetic field. Neurotransmitters are the body's chemical messengers that allow neurons (nerve cells) to communicate with each other, across a tiny gap called a synapse. They regulate both physical and psychological functions.

So, what is the role of spirituality in the bio-electromagnetic field of human existence?

Firstly, the human body has its own magnetic fields. The human heart produces an electric current that runs through the body and to every cell. This electric current in the body generates an electro-magnetic field. The function of the bio-electromagnetic field in the human body is to transmit messages from one part of the body to another, through neurons, the messenger cells in the nervous system. These are the electrical signals carrying messages through the nerve impulses.

When I first saw my dad lying in bed, unresponsive, my brain sensed impending cessation of life, and then when I received the message that he had taken his final breath and was no more, the shock produced an electric current that ran through my body, to every cell, triggering an acute stress response which altered the electrical and magnetic rhythms of both my heart and my brain, causing a surge in stress hormones, like cortisol and adrenalin. Thus, my body's electromagnetic field became disrupted, shifting from a coherent pattern to an incoherent erratic pattern. This incoherence quickly disrupted my nervous system, from being calm to becoming mentally paralysed as I tried to process the distressing information. This is what felt like a psychological tornado that created instability in the internal atmosphere of my being.

Positive emotions like love and compassion produce coherent patterns while negative emotions like fear and anger, create erratic incoherent and weaker signals. Research also suggests that memories of emotions that are stored within the body's electromagnetic fields, act as an energetic storage system where unresolved emotions are associated with disrupted coherence. Positive emotional states promote coherence between the heart, brain, and nervous system, leading to improved cognitive function and health.

Negative emotions increase stress hormones like cortisol and affect the body's overall electromagnetic energy and can potentially lead to hypervigilance, anxiety, depression and/or decreased immune function which means, a poor defence mechanism against illnesses and in extreme cases, auto-immune disease. Research has demonstrated that spiritual practice is the most effective way to reduce cortisol levels, as this will help develop the body's resilience against physical and mental ill-health.

It is evident here that the biology and neurology of the human body are systemically interconnected, for protection against ill-health. However, if the 'human spirit' is a non-physical entity, that cannot be measured with neurological data, I am intrigued as to how it became part of a structured system, responsible for overall wellbeing, within the human body.

The human brain is not just a generator of thoughts but an antenna that connects human beings to a larger shared and meaningful cosmos through spirituality as an innate capacity to perceive that individuals are part of a single, greater whole

8. What is 'Spirit'

The only things in life that compatibly exist with this grand universe are the creative works of the human spirit

'Spirit' usually means the essential, non-physical element or inner character of a living being. It is the psyche, the immaterial part of a human being, the vital life force that continues after death. The word 'spirit' originates from the Latin word 'spiritus' and is related to the verb 'spirare' which means "to breathe." In the mid 13th century, it meant 'respiration' or 'breath of life', in other words, life itself, as there is no life without breath.

The word 'psychology' originates from the Greek word 'psyche', which means 'soul'. The soul is defined as one's consciousness; one's life force and is at the core of one's being. The soul, as illustrated above, is what is constituted by the spirit and by and large, the spiritual dimension of one's existence. Thus 'psychology' is the study of the human soul, one's inner being, one's consciousness, the very essence.

Consciousness is the subjective moment to moment awareness of oneself, environment, including thoughts, sensations, feelings and memories. It combines external sensory information with internal mental processes.

Studies suggest that consciousness exists both in deep sleep and in a state of unarousable unresponsiveness, even if unable to move or speak. In a study in 2023, Columbia researchers identified patients with hidden consciousness who could hear and comprehend verbal commands but could not carry them out due to dysfunctional brain circuits.

So, how does the concept of spirituality explain that the 'spirit' is the 'breath of life' that has come to be the realm of consciousness in man, his very life force?

The only evidence consistent with the meaning of soul and spirit, both philosophically and scientifically, is found in the very first book of the Holy Bible:

And the LORD God formed man of the dust of the earth and breathed into his nostrils the breath of life; and man became a living soul. Genesis 2:7

This is a clear demonstration of the breath of God encompassing the soul that makes man a 'living soul'. In essence a living soul is the conscious entity of a person, body, mind, and spirit, functioning in the physical world through the divine breath of the Creator.

But how do we know that the Holy Bible is an original documentation of historical events?

The 66 books of the Bible written over one thousand five hundred years, by over forty authors from different backgrounds, maintains a consistent message, presenting a cohesive picture of God's plan for humanity.

It is evidence-based knowledge that thousands of Greek manuscripts of the New-Testament still exist, and the Dead Sea scrolls show that old-testament texts were copied with high accuracy over centuries, and this is proof that the Bible is the best-preserved ancient text. Non-Christian sources such as Tacitus refer to Jesus' execution under Pilate. Josephus mentions Jesus and early Christians.

Back in the very 1st century, a limestone bone box was discovered with the inscription "James, son of Joseph, brother of Jesus". This is called The James Ossuary. Mathew 13: 55 reads *Is not this, the carpenter, son of Mary and Joseph and brother of James, Joses, Judas and Simon?* In 1990, an ornate bone box was found in Jerusalem, containing the inscription, "Joseph son of Caiaphas" identifying the High Priest who delivered

Jesus to Pilate. This is called the Caiaphas Ossuary. History records Joseph Caiaphas as the Jewish high priest from A.D. 18-36, known for presiding over the Sanhedrin trial that condemned Jesus to death. This is documented in the Bible in Mathew 26:57 & John 18:13-28. Even without archaeological discoveries, substantial historical evidence from secular sources supports the existence of Jesus of Nazareth.

The traditional western calendar has been divided based on Jesus' birth and death. BC, (ante Christum in Latin) which means 'before Christ' and AD, (anno domini, in Latin) as, in the year of the Lord, referring to the era following the estimated birth of Jesus Christ. AD counts years forward from year 1, and BC counts backward.

This decodes any complexity around the fact that the Bible, as an ancient scripture is not only historical and supported archaeologically but because its text shows a high degree of consistency, and predictions made in the old-testament have been fulfilled in the new-testament. Prophecies concerning global conflict and instability that were made in the Bible thousands of years ago (*There will be wars and rumours of wars, Mathew 24:6); (Nation will rise against nation, and kingdom against kingdom: and there shall be earthquakes in divers' places, and famines and troubles: Mark 13:8)* are unfolding before our eyes today. The escalation of wars, global division, natural disasters and pandemics are emerging in plain sight.

The prophet Jeremiah prophesied of Elam (Iran) in the Old Testament:

Behold, I will break the bow of Elam, the foremost of their might. Against Elam I will bring the four winds from the four quarters of Heaven and scatter them toward all those winds. There shall be no nations where the outcasts of Elam will not go. For I will cause Elam to be dismayed before their enemies and before those who seek their life. I will bring disaster upon them. My fierce anger, says the Lord, I will send the sword after them, until I have consumed them. I will set my throne in Elam, and will destroy from there, the king and the princes. But it shall come to pass, in the latter days, I will bring back the captives and the exiles, sayeth the Lord God Almighty. Jeremiah 49: 34 - 39

Elam in the Old Testament refers to present-day southwestern Iran. The 'broken bow' of Elam is interpreted as the weakening of modern Iran's military power, specifically its nuclear ambitions. The above passage in the Bible prophesies restoration both, of the captives and the exiles.

Although science is agnostic about biblical events, there is adequate historic and archeological evidence to prove that God is not a philosophical proposition. There is no direct archeological artifact of Jesus himself but there is strong historical evidence from multiple sources that Jesus lived and was crucified.

Dr Van Deurzen's statement: *When people rediscover their inner connectedness to something greater than themselves, to some ideal which will lift them beyond their everyday struggles, a new motivation flows inside of them, which can carry them through difficulties with unerring purposefulness,* suggests that the one source of energy that offers human beings the motivation to overcome their life challenges is their inner 'soul' connection to the higher power, but that this would have to be rediscovered. This implies that a connection has pre-existed and has got to be discovered and reclaimed. The Bible explains this pre-existing connection in the story of creation.

Firstly, what is this higher power? What do we mean by 'transcendence'?

Scientists like Carl Sagan and Albert Einstein spoke of the 'higher power' not as a deity, but as the awe-inspiring, overarching mysteries and laws of the Universe. Einstein described this as a cosmic religious feeling which he considered the driving force behind all pioneering scientific research.

The word 'transcendence' is derived from the Latin meaning 'to climb beyond', referring to moving past physical constraints to experience a higher connectivity or divinity. Divinity is defined as the essence of God, supreme being or a sacred power.

Abraham Maslow, the founder of humanistic psychology, who developed the theory of hierarchy of needs, states that 'transcendence' is the state where an individual's consciousness extends beyond personal needs to connect deeply with nature, the cosmos, and the well-being of others.

Science defines divinity, not as a verifiable physical entity but as a concept arising from human consciousness, cognitive faculties, emotional, psychological, or spiritual experiences of nature. Science interprets divinity through fields of psychology and neurology. The science of divinity attempts to combine consciousness or the 'spirit' with physics to define divinity as the objective reality found within the structure of the universe, rather than a supernatural being. Is it possible then, that an intricately designed universe with the complexity of its design as we know it, could exist without the divine intervention of a power, higher than creation itself?

Physicist Lawrence Krauss suggests that physical laws can give rise to something without any external cause. He states that quantum fields and gravity are enough for something to emerge, without the need for someone to create something. Quantum fields are not created, rather they are fundamental components of the universe, existing everywhere throughout spacetime as the underlying reality from which particles emerge. This implies that, quantum fields as quantum physics explains it, pre-existed.

Kris Franken, in her article 'The Spiritual Big Bang-the birth of Souls' states: *The Universe did not come into existence from a literal, chaotic 'nothingness' or an empty void but rather emerged from a fullness of non-material potentiality, often described as infinite consciousness, love, or the divine mind.* This is not difficult to comprehend because it is illogical to believe that 'something can be produced from nothing'. Only nothing can be produced from nothing. The outcome of nothing is nothing.

According to quantum physics, however, something can be produced from nothing because 'nothing' is not an absolute void. It refers to a quantum vacuum wherein is a bubbling cauldron of energy, confirming that matter can be created from empty space, provided there is an underlying energy. Time, Space and the Universe, we know has not always existed, but the spirit of God as a source of underlying energy, has. This is consistent with the Bible: *In the beginning, God created the Heaven and the Earth. And the earth was without form and void; and darkness was upon the face of the deep. And the spirit of God moved upon the face of the waters. Genesis 1:1-2*

The Bible is not a scientific textbook, but a spiritual text which has historically been a source of divine wisdom, comfort and moral direction. It is considered, the most read, sold, published, best-selling book in the world. Its language and description of divine activity prove that perceivable reality is not observable through human eyes. The spirit world is not seen but perceived and experienced by faith. *By faith, we understand that the Universe was formed at God's command, so that, what is seen was not made out of what was visible. Hebrews 11:3*

The breath of God is presented in theological and biblical contexts as the primary conduit of life and the divine spark that connects humanity to its Creator. It represents not only the physical animation, but the infusion of 'Spirit' (Ruach, the Greek translation) connecting the finite human to the infinite God. Unlike other creatures spoken into existence (And God said, *let there be light and there was light, Genesis 1:3*) humanity received this direct, personal contact (the breath of life), signifying a unique connection to God. *But it is the spirit in a person, the breath of the Almighty, that gives them understanding. Job 32:8*

If creation is an unalterable truth, so is the 'breath of God' (the human spirit) as the source of human consciousness and the innate capacity to know, seek and understand things in the divine sphere of existence. When human beings breathe, they are sustained and continue to be sustained by the breath (spirit) that came from God.

Kris Franken emphasises on the breath of God in reality, as being, the spiritual big bang which is the concept that the universe's origin was the moment 'consciousness' or a 'divine force' expanded into matter, creating the cosmos out of nothing, an intentional and creative act where divine energy manifested into existence.

God spoke the Universe into existence, but the 'big bang' has acted as a quantum mechanism theory that gives existence a scientific framework. God, the higher power, the big banger made the big bang to happen. According to quantum field theory, fundamental fields do not need to be created as they are considered pre-existing, foundational components of the universe that existed everywhere, even in a vacuum. When something pre-exists, it means that it existed in a former state, a different state. A piece of wooden furniture, for example, pre-existed as a tree, so also, the universe.

This is evident in the Bible:

In the beginning, God created the heavens and the earth. Now, the earth was formless and empty, darkness was over the surface of the deep, and the Spirit of God, hovered over the waters. And God said, "Let there be light" and there was light. God saw that the light was good and He separated the light from darkness. God called the light, day and the darkness, He called night. And there was evening, and there was morning, the first day. Genesis 1:1-5

So, the spirit of God that pre-existed, hovered over the waters, before the heavens and the earth came into being, and subsequently, God breathed His breath into the man, He created from the dust of the earth, and thus, creation emerged. The concept that the breath of God produced vibrations that created the universe, is a significant theme within mystical, theological and spiritual interpretations, bridging the gap between ancient sacred texts and modern concepts of energy.

Thus, the universe is not just a container of particles, it is a collection of interconnected, vibrating quantum fields that constitute the very fabric of reality. The spirit of God, therefore, was the vibrating movement, the divine energy that brought life to inert matter. His breath was the divine command that animated the inanimate, setting the cosmos into motion. God, the prime mover, imparted energy in the form of waves (sound, light and heat) into the universe.

So, if the breath of God(spirit) made man into a living (soul), then, they (spirit & soul) should have to work in unison. Are their functions interchangeable?

> **'Spirit' is the essence of consciousness, the energy of the Universe that creates all things.**

9. Soul vs Spirit

The soul is an animating, moral spirit, the self-reflecting, truth-discerning essence that elevates individuals above the animal world.

It seems that we sometimes refer to the 'soul' without a clear understanding of what it really is. This is because the soul does not bear a physical structure and cannot be verified anatomically.

The soul is said to be the seat of personality, thoughts, emotions and what makes a person unique.

Plato (428–347 BC), the ancient Greek philosopher from Athens, student of Socrates, and teacher of Aristotle, who shaped Western philosophy, metaphysics, and ethics through his written dialogues, states that the soul is the essence of a person, tied to purpose and identity.

The Latin translation for the word 'soul' is 'anima' which Carl Jung's Analytical psychology interprets as one's inner self, or the 'vital life force', without which one cannot develop one's authentic self.

The Greek translation for the word spirit is 'pneuma' which means 'breath of life' or the vital life force, denoting the immaterial aspect of humanity. The Bible refers to 'spirit' as the breath, the life force, the divine power or presence, the inner being that connects one to God, through a consciousness of the higher power. It is the unique ability to comprehend and understand things beyond the human intellect.

Plato's idea of spirit (*thymus*) maps well onto some concepts in psychology, as the emotional, high-spirited part of the soul responsible for anger, indignation, courage, and the drive for honour or victory. Consequently, the soul is one's essence at the core of oneself, and the spirit, the life force. The essence of a human being is the life force and therefore, the function of the soul and spirit are inseparably connected.

Neuroscience expounds the human spirit as experiences of spirituality, consciousness, and self, as emergent properties of brain activity rather than an immaterial entity. Key brain regions like the temporal region, responsible for meaning & emotion; parietal region, responsible for self & space; and frontal lobes responsible for attention & intent; collaborate to create feelings of unity, self-awareness and transcendence. It treats spiritual experiences as neural processes that can be activated by meditation and/or prayer.

Existential Philosophy explains the human spirit as a deliberate, creative radiance produced through the freedom, resilience, and conscious choices of the individual. It offers the capacity to create meaning and purpose in life.

Quantum Physics elucidates that the human spirit is a deeper, non-physical component, but the very essence of human existence. It illustrates the soul as the message, content, or information of a quantum vibrational field. It explains that the soul (information) guides the spiritual heart (reception), which tells the mind (processing) where to direct energy to create or transform matter. It posits that the soul may persist beyond physical death.

According to the Quantum Theory of Soul, when a person experiences clinical death, the quantum information that forms their consciousness is not destroyed and as a result, this information leaves the physical body and disperses into the universe, which explains the concept of the soul being immortal. The Bible speaks of the soul as 'immortal'; however, it is not inherently immortal but is dependent on its belief and connection with God, the higher power, for eternal life. *For God so loved the world, that He gave His only begotten Son, that whosoever believeth in Him, should not perish but have eternal life. John 3:16.*

Several parts of my conscious self, felt fragmented the day my grief over losing my father compounded the loss of my mother, but I know that it was the breath of my Creator within, that held the promise of re-integrating my broken parts, creating a new sense of wholeness. I do not believe this was a conscious process, but somehow, I seem to have found meaning in the face of absurdity, integration in the face of severance of the most valuable, crucial attachments I have ever had.

As days and weeks went by, I discovered that I continued to exist, because my spirit, soul and body re-integrated through my conscious connection with the one who created me. However, I also uncovered the truth that just as the body requires food to fuel its physical existence, the spirit too needs to be activated and sustained.

According to Dr David Richo, a psychotherapist, *the 'givens' of life are the unavoidable realities of human existence that, when accepted, rather than resisted, lead to greater emotional peace and resilience.* A lack of inner peace would mean, a lack of change and growth. I have inquired and investigated but find no explanation other than my connection and relationship with that higher power, that helped me accept the loss of my pain to find the peace I desired for. The peace I now have is a consequence of my belief that God, our Creator, not only created us human beings to enjoy life here on this mortal earth but has instituted eternal life. This belief can be validated by the first law of 'Thermodynamics', which posits that energy cannot be created or destroyed, only transformed. Identically, if the human spirit (the breath of the Creator) is the energy that cannot be destroyed, then it can only be transformed.

I have been able to experience this transformation, as I dug my feet into the sand even when it kept shifting under my feet; my heart was able to perceive, even when my eyes dimmed my vision, through my tears; my brain was able to fathom the reality of the sustenance of the soul after the loss of life and the pain of my loss felt insurmountable. It was my soul, the divine power of the presence of the one who created me, intricately designed to provide the vital life force, that enabled a comprehension of purpose in this life and the hope for eternity.

I see the compelling energy of my spirit, the breath of God, knitted together with the consciousness in my soul, that empowers me each day, to rise with strength and motivation, to walk towards the fulfilment of my life's purpose. *For you created my inmost being, you knit me together in my mother's womb. I praise you because I am fearfully and wonderfully made. Your works are wonderful and that, my soul knows well. Psalm 139:13-14.*

Despite my unshakeable belief and the connection, I have with my Creator, I cannot stop wondering if I continue to exist, masking a belief that all is well while the wound of my grief in my soul is quietly festering, beneath the hustle and bustle of my everyday life.

Can the loss of a parent wound one's soul? If so, how about the other losses, loss of a child, loss of a sibling or spouse, loss of a job or a house, loss of trust, security and reality when one is betrayed, robbed, rejected, abandoned, abused, violated or traumatised in some way?

Soul wounds are believed to be deep emotional, mental and spiritual injuries caused by unresolved trauma, abuse or even intense adverse life circumstances.

They are said to distort a person's perception, personality and relationships, causing them to erect unhealthy walls with a view to protect self from further hurt and pain. When loss of a loved one is compounded by early life trauma, burying the unresolved pain can almost be an unconscious act.

In my work as a psychotherapist, I help my patients unearth any un-addressed, unresolved tragedy and their traumatic response, with the aim of helping them confront the emotional pain they inadvertently stored away, as this is what causes wounding in the depths of one's being.

A human being is a spirit who possesses a soul and lives in a body. Health is the state of harmony of the body, mind, soul and spirit.

10. Soul Wounds

The wound is the place where light enters you

A wound is a physical injury that breaks the skin, often resulting from trauma, accidents or medical procedures. Physical wounds are tangible and are easy to treat.

According to psychology, soul wounds are deep emotional/psychological injuries that can cause one to disconnect from a sense of self, manifesting pain-based identities, when one allows the painful experiences to define self, as a victim, or broken, or as ashamed, unworthy, inferior, a failure, un-loveable, un-attractive or never good enough. Soul wounds are neither visible nor tangible. They are not abstract ideas or imaginary concepts either. An example of what could cause wounds in one's soul could be the emotional response to a statement such as 'Can you never ever get anything right?'.

When facing severe emotional pain, physical abuse, or neglect, the mind can switch off from reality, creating a distance between the person and their experiences, thereby causing a disconnection from self. Disconnection from self does not always mean 'broken' but can indicate a protective coping mechanism used by the mind to manage trauma or overwhelming emotions.

Psychology defines 'brokenness' as a felt experience of being shattered to the point where there is no guarantee that the pieces can be put back together. It is a crushing of the spirit, caused by acute trauma that can cause fragmentation of memories, eventually, fragmentation of self or a disconnection from one's real self because they no longer feel worthy or deserving of life.

My sense of 'feeling shattered' is certainly making me wonder if I too have been crushed in my spirit but managed to bury my injuries so no one will know just how vulnerable it made me feel.

In examining the dimensions of existence (refer chapter five), it is evident that the soul, is, in fact, insulated by the physical, the social and the emotional layers of existence. Therefore, the soul is only harmed if we engage with and believe in the contradictory voice of the enemy of our soul.

The enemy of our soul is our spiritual adversary, the evil one and his forces, seeking to induce fear, cause hopelessness, powerlessness, and despair. The lies of the enemy of our soul are those intrusive thoughts such as 'God can never love you', 'you have nothing to give because you have lost everything'; 'you will never amount to anything'; 'you are empty and unworthy'; 'people hurt you because you are weak and cannot stand up for yourself'; 'your suffering will never end and you will never make it'; 'you may as well quit'; 'you are powerless, just give up'.

Once we agree with these lies, we align with the objective of the enemy, who will then make us question and doubt our gifts, our talents, our strengths, our core potential, our sense of self, the very essence of our being. We begin to feel defective and worthless because we have no power to fight the enemy. If our 'self' is our 'soul', then our belief of our 'self', on account of life's losses, or abuse or trauma, can allow a wounding of our soul, the deepest innermost part of 'self'.

The way we allow for soul wounds is through 'belief'. This may be referred to as a distorted belief. However, our human 'spirit', the breath of life, God breathed into each one of us, that made us into a living soul, is indestructible, imperishable, invincible, impenetrable as it is 'immortal'. As I process this in my inner-being, I comprehend that my soul cannot be wounded because I have denied entry to all the distorted beliefs that tried to permeate. I recognise that for as long as I refuse to believe the enemy of my soul, my soul will remain unscathed. Wounds can be inflicted but they cannot penetrate the soul because it was made to remain, to exist beyond this life. The essence of existence is in the meaning it creates and the only meaning existence can create is in its connection to the divine, according to philosophical and scientific thinking, which is in perfect alignment with the Biblical concept of eternal life. *To them who by patient continuance in well-doing seek for glory and honour and immortality, eternal life. Romans 2: 7*

If the essence of existence is in the meaning it can create, then there is no adversity or tragedy that can cause dysfunction within our human structure, both in the natural and spiritual realms. The Bible states that *All things work together for good to them that love God, to them who are the called according to His purpose. Romans 8:28.* This is attributed to the origin of God's creation that had meaning and purpose before man's existence, as revealed in His word: *Before I formed you in the womb, I knew you. Before you were born, I set you apart. Jeremiah 1:5*

A new-born baby is wrapped up warm to be protected from any contaminants in the air but will not be placed in his crib to rest until he is placed in his mother's arms to be nourished and nurtured. Similarly, the soul, just by virtue of pre-existence does not automatically nourish itself. The soul needs to remain connected with its Creator, for nourishment, strength, and growth, diligently seeking to walk in righteousness. *So that as sin reigned in death, even so grace might reign through righteousness to eternal life through Jesus Christ our Lord. Romans 5:21*

When the human soul is wounded, it becomes susceptible to vulnerability which then becomes breeding ground for both mental and physical dysfunction. If, for example, fear as an emotion is programmed into our nervous system for a survival instinct, to protect ourselves from danger, it is healthy. However, a spirit of fear caused by abuse or gross neglect, that renders powerlessness; a loss of capacity to think, reason and understand; can weaken the immune system; cause cardiovascular damage and gastrointestinal issues.

When God created the heavens and the earth, He established human existence on the earth, instituting the laws of well-being. Here is the most important law: *For God hath not given us the spirit of fear; but of power, of love, and of a sound mind. 2 Timothy 1:7*

Scientific evidence demonstrates that the human brain is wired for love, through a complex interplay of reward circuitry, neurotransmitters and specialised hormone systems that promote bonding through relationships, pleasure and survival.

While human beings are born with a predisposition to fear certain threats like snakes, spiders or loud noises, through the brain's alarm centres, research suggests that most fears are typically activated through environmental cues rather than being inherited at birth. This affirms the truth that God did not give us a spirit of fear. Thus 'fear' is not a given, it is learned.

Therefore, the only way to build resilience and heal the wounds of the soul is to re-discover and re-establish the connection with that higher power that enables a spirit of love, power and a sound mind. However, re-establishing that connection with the higher power, is an intentional choice.

The choices we make, fundamentally depend on our 'belief', which act as the operating system for the mind as they shape our values and define what we see as possible. I do believe in the infinite power of my Creator, but I wonder why I sometimes fail to believe in myself, His creation. What is it that causes me to believe or to not believe?

A wounded soul is a state of being that has experienced a significant decrease in love, harmony, acceptance and a significant increase in strife, discord and resistance

11. Belief

It is this belief in a power larger than myself and other than myself which allows me to venture into the unknown and even the unknowable

The pain of losing my parents shattered me enough to step into a deep dark hole of distress. Darkness cannot destroy light but is the absence of light. Choosing to disconnect myself from my responsibilities and just stay afloat with no direction, would mean I choose to remain in the darkness of the hole that will render my very journey of life, purposeless. It felt like that was a reasonable option, to protect myself from other gale winds I imagined, could strike. However, it also meant that I would have no sense of security as life is one of uncertainty and I will have to venture into the unknown. This would leave me feeling empty, stripping my life of meaning. I chose instead, to choose light.

I sensed, in my soul, a consistent urge to direct the 'energy' I had within, to re-create new meaning, to transform the 'matter' of my loss. This is the light, I know, can destroy the darkness of distress. Here was the interaction between energy and matter. Enabling the energy in my soul, my inner being, to interact with my loss, would mean that I will find a way to heal my 'inner self'. To do this, I had to intentionally dismantle my distorted belief that I was depleted, inadequate or that I no longer had a sense of identity and a reason to carry on. Here is an illustration of how 'belief' impacts the soul:

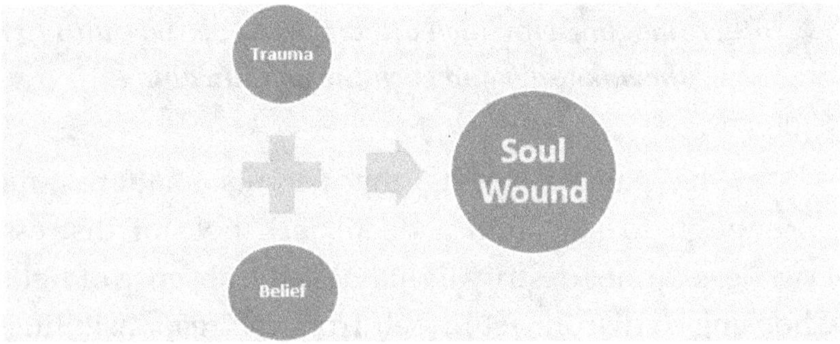

Trauma, as commonly understood, is not the tragic event or the deeply painful incident. Trauma is the emotional response to a deeply distressing or life-threatening event that overwhelms one's capacity to cope as it shatters the sense of safety. This then can disrupt the very fundamental assumptions or beliefs about oneself, the world and life. A soul wound therefore is a function of the combination of the deeply distressing event and the disrupted belief. However, when the distorted beliefs are reframed and restructured, then soul wounds can be healed and restored.

How is it that 'belief' can make such a profound difference? What really is a belief?

A 'belief' is a subjective conviction that something is true, real or exists, often based on a personal or cultural framework for interpreting the world. Beliefs do not require proof, they can be based on faith, experience or assumption; faith on someone we love and trust.

A belief can be said to be the very foundation of personal reality. It acts as a self-fulfilling prophecy that shapes our actions and potential. Believing in self, is critical to establishing a self-concept. Key insights emphasise that believing in yourself, your abilities and dreams, is crucial to unlocking your potential, while also noting that beliefs can dictate your limits or set you free.

Beliefs can change brain chemistry almost instantaneously. They trigger the release of endorphins, a natural morphine produced by the body, to align the brain's internal state with what it believed to be happening. Endorphins are powerful neurotransmitters. According to research from the McKinsey Health Institute, frontiers in Behavioural Neuroscience, 'beliefs' are associated with reward-related brain regions and 'disbelief' is associated with areas linked to emotional conflict. So, if I believe that I am inadequate, or that I will always be a failure, my lack of belief in myself can leave me feeling deeply conflicted. Consistent internal conflict can trigger stress hormones, namely cortisol. High cortisol can lead to high blood pressure, diabetes, muscle weakness and inflammation in the body. Prolonged exposure to cortisol can lead to depression, anxiety, severe mood swings and cognitive deficits. (referenced in chapter seven) Distorted beliefs, according to Harvard Health, negatively impact mental health by creating irrational, habitual thought patterns that fuel anxiety, depression, low self-esteem, and relational issues. These mental filters skew perception, leading to excessive worry, hopelessness and behaviours like social withdrawal or self-defeating actions.

It is fascinating how a simple act of belief can influence emotional, mental, and spiritual wellbeing by acting as a filter that shapes personal reality providing a sense of meaning and purpose. Positive, deeply held beliefs can increase happiness, reduce stress, and improve the overall wellbeing through feelings of hope, optimism, and compassion.

I can choose to believe in my ability to remain resilient, in my capacity to change and grow, by finding meaning through my loss. This is how I can protect my soul from being wounded. From a physiological perspective, the soul is insulated and not directly exposed to external danger. However internalising mental conflicts that produce a distorted belief, reduce self-esteem, causing psychological wounds in the soul.

Daniel Kahneman states, *that for our most important beliefs, we have no evidence at all, except that people we love and trust, hold these beliefs.* What happens to our belief system when we lose the people we loved and trusted? We can of course, choose to continue to believe but our belief then will have no basis or point of origin. Could we instead, choose to love and trust our Creator who not only created the earth and the universe in all its splendour but also designed every human being in His own image, as documented in the Bible: *So, God created mankind in His own image, in the image of God, created He them, Genesis 1:27;* then we have a clear understanding of our origin, an established sense of identity and a basis for our belief. The scripture goes on to define the outcome of belief as the source of life itself. *He that believeth on me, as the scripture hath said, out of his belly shall flow rivers of living water John 7:38.*

This implies that when 'belief in God' is derived from within the 'Soul' (breath of God), it prompts the outflow of the river of living water, in other words, the very source of life. What is noteworthy here is that the river of living water is pre-existent in every individual by virtue of the breath of God. A failure to believe could result with a lack of consciousness of one's core potential without which meaning and purpose cannot be derived.

The human soul was designed to remain resilient and re-generate new meaning, but it can do so, only when nurtured and nourished. It cannot disintegrate when nurtured and nourished. Finding a renewed purpose, strengthens man, rewires the mind, restores the spirit, and propels one to move forward.

It is not enough that we believe in a higher power. We need to be connected to this divine power of God himself. We need to believe in who He has made us to be. We need to trust in the process He will take us through, to help us become, the individuals He designed us to be.

I recognise the need to allow my faith in myself through my faith in my Creator, to emerge from within my soul, to spring forth, to produce light from darkness, so my spirit can be regenerated with an intentional determination, not just to remain grounded, but to rise, to move, to run, until I arrive at the finish line.

'To believe' in the Creator, is not about religion. It is about a relationship with the one who breathed the breath of life. It is about re-establishing the pre-existing connection. It is the one relationship that will stand the test of time, help overcome the existential anxieties of life and heal the wounds of the soul, offering wholesome well-being and the hope of eternal life. The pre-existing connection with the Creator, through the 'breath of life' is that divine connection that triggers feelings of profound peace and unconditional love.

But the question I need to ask myself is, how does belief in the one who breathed His breath into me, activate my spirit to be able to see my faith at work?

The root of belief is faith. Faith is the core of spirituality. To believe therefore, is a function of the spirit.

12. Shattered but Unscathed – a Spiritual Perspective

Faith is the strength by which a shattered world shall emerge into light

In my quest to comprehend the impact of the tornado that struck me, I recognise the need to find solid ground beneath the shifting sand of what I believed to be the process of grieving. I was well versed with the stages of grief but that knowledge neither grounded me nor healed the pain of my grief.

I recall the words of the hymn writer Edward Mote, a British cabinet maker, around 1834:

On Christ the solid rock I stand
All other ground is sinking sand
All other ground is sinking sand

When darkness veils His lovely face
I rest on His unchanging grace
In every high and stormy gale
My anchor holds within the veil

His oath, His covenant, His blood
Support me in the whelming flood
When all around my soul gives way
He then is all my hope and stay

In a world of uncertainty, where life does not permit us to choose our givens, we need the solidarity of a power above the power of this natural realm, the rock that we can rely on. Our human connections, our financial status, our education, our societal position, everything we ever accomplished, our accolades, will one day, fail to sustain the security they offered. They will one day, prove to be sinking sand. Our ultimate security is in our Creator because the one who breathed His breath into us and made us living souls, has everything we will ever need, for our well-being, both naturally and spiritually. However, we cannot access His provision and protection unless we remain connected with Him. *I am the vine; you are the branches. He who abides in Me, and I in Him, bears much fruit; for without Me, you can do nothing. John 15:5*

The loss of my parents threatened to drown me in the grief I struggled to make sense of, but as I found my feet on the solid rock of my faith in my Creator, I found my anchor, my one true source of strength and hope.

The Bible documents a storm in Mark 4:38-41. A storm of wind caused the waves to beat into the ship, that Jesus and His disciples were in, so that the water was quickly filling in. Jesus then rebuked the wind and said to the sea *Peace be still.* Immediately the winds ceased and the sea calmed down. Then Jesus asked His disciples why they were so fearful and if they had lost their faith. Here is how the Bible defines faith: *Now faith is the substance of things hoped for, the evidence of things not seen. Hebrews 11:1.*

Jesus points out here that the only way to remain fearless amid a storm that is threatening to engulf, is through faith. The faith Jesus expected in His disciples, was in His ability to calm the sea. The problem here seems to be that Jesus' disciples at the time, had not got to know Him well enough to believe in His power and control over all His creation. *I will set him on high because he hath known my name. Psalm 91:14b.* We have the assurance of God that by virtue of knowing Him, we can remain unscathed. It is not difficult to put our faith and trust in someone we know, in the consciousness of our spirit.

'Faith' as is evident here is not a passive belief, but an active, spiritual principle by which people live, guiding them to trust in something beyond tangible proof, the force that helps connect with that higher being, to find meaning and navigate life's challenges. It is the foundational component of the spiritual dimension of human existence.

However, the only way to develop faith in a God that cannot be seen with human eyes, is to get to know

Him, through studying and engaging with the spiritual texts, the Bible, to converse with God through prayer and meditation, as the Bible says, *In the beginning, was the word, and the word was with God and the word was God. John 1:1.* Through engaging with His word, we are also able to stay focused and remain grounded, in times of difficulty, crisis and challenge. It is written in *Isaiah 26:3 You will keep him in perfect peace, whose mind is stayed on you.*

Now, this is the key to entering into and remaining in the eye of the storm, using our mind to maintain focus on the words of the creator himself. It is the focus of the human mind on the infinite power of the divine. It is this point of convergence of the human and the divine, that forms the tranquil centre, the place where human anxiety is exchanged for divine peace.

A comprehension of the dimensions of existence and a perception of the mastermind of the Creator of the Universe who not only pre-designed and established human existence on the earth but intricately interlinked the functions of the earth and existence of mankind on the earth, can effectively enable every individual to navigate life's journey, with passion and purpose. *For in Him, we live, and move, and have our being; for we are His offspring. Acts 17:28*

Human intellect cannot perceive nor comprehend the works of the Creator, the higher power. God breathed His breath into man so His spirit would become part of humanity, forming the human spirit. This then made man into a living 'soul'. However, in order for the human spirit to lift us beyond our everyday challenges and carry us through some of life's painful givens, it needs daily activation. It is written: *This book of law shall not depart out of your mouth; you shall meditate on it day and night, that you may observe to do according to all that is written therein: for then, you shall make your way prosperous, and have good success. Joshua 1:8*

The function of the human being as a holistic triad of body, mind, and soul, represents the physical, cognitive, and spiritual dimensions. The body acts as the physical vessel, the mind encompasses intellect and emotions, but the spirit and soul serve as the inner essence, through consciousness, connecting to the divine, through the word of God. The mind bridges the gap between the physical body and the spiritual essence.

'Consciousness' as a function of man's soul, does not make him immune to life's tragedies and traumatic responses. The only way to remain resistant is to stay connected to the soul of the divine. It is written in Psalm 34:18, *The Lord is close to the broken hearted and saves those who are crushed in the spirit.* Psalm 147:3 says: *He heals the broken hearted and binds up their wounds.*

There is no human being upon the face of the earth, who has not experienced failure, loss, deep disappointment, tragedy or been pained in some way. *We are hard-pressed on every side but not crushed;*

perplexed, but not in despair; persecuted but not abandoned; struck down but not destroyed. 2 Corinthians 4:8-9. God in His sovereignty, has made every provision through His word, for His children, to remain rooted and grounded in faith.

The catalyst for healing and resolution of the wounds that life's givens can produce deep down in our souls, as human beings, is 'faith' through our 'belief' in God, in His word. Research indicates that 'belief' acts as a powerful catalyst by transforming personal identity, driving behavioural change, and fostering resilience during crises. Deeply held spiritual beliefs catalyse positive life changes, reduce uncertainty, and foster post-traumatic growth.

From a scientific perspective, it is widely acknowledged that belief in God is believed to heal deep 'soul wounds', invisible emotional, spiritual, and psychological pain. It provides comfort, purpose, and a sense of being loved. Through belief which produces faith, individuals find restoration, replacing fear with peace, and finding meaning in suffering, often viewing God as a source of healing that restores what was broken.

Faith, which is rooted in belief, helps individuals shift their identity from that of a victim to that of an overcomer, replacing feelings of worthlessness with a sense of being valued, increasing their self-worth.

Rather than hiding emotional wounds, 'belief' allows exposure and healing, thereby precipitating growth and maturity.

Feeling shattered is feeling broken on the inside. But this state of brokenness, a sense of being cracked open, has not only exposed my vulnerability, but uncovered my sense of inadequacy, allowing the light of the strength, grace and wisdom of my Creator, to make me into a conduit of light, shattering the darkness of hopelessness, producing a persistent courage to stand intact, whole and complete.

'Kintsugi' is a Japanese art that repairs broken pottery with gold, rendering a new piece that is more exquisite than it was before the break. It literally means 'to join with gold'.

"Rather than trying to hide the damage, kintsugi highlights the repair. The imperfections are what make it beautiful and valuable. A broken piece that is put back together has more of a story, is more authentic and real, stronger and more resilient than something that has stayed pristine". *To appoint unto them that mourn in Zion, to give unto them beauty for ashes, the oil of joy for mourning, the garment of praise for the spirit of heaviness; that they might be called trees of righteousness, the planting of the Lord, that he might be glorified. Isaiah 61:3*

I did not know that the pain of my LOSS could help me GAIN more VALUE

I did not know the ASHES of my SUFFERING could produce BEAUTY and JOY

I know I was SHATTERED, but I remain UNSCATHED, BROKEN yet WHOLE

I now COME FORTH, with the hope of BRINGING LIGHT, I EXIST with PURPOSE

Epilogue

Writing this book has been an exciting journey for me, as I did not envisage, the depth of learning, I have personally gained from the direction it has taken. It has been an honour to use the story of my grief, backed by science and philosophy to comprehend the framework of human existence in the light of the dimensions of the earth, with a view to get to know the magnificent Creator of the Universe.

A few days after my dad passed away, one of my friends kept checking in on me, asking how I was. I felt very touched by his concern and wrote back "shattered but at peace". Not long after sending that response, I felt like the title of this book 'Shattered but unscathed' became visible to me in my mind's eye and landed in my spirit. This is when I knew, I was being summoned, to write this book. A few weeks later, another friend wrote, asking how I was, and I wrote back "there is a time when you allow tears to roll down your cheeks, then there is the time they roll out of your heart which only God can see, so He sends loving souls like you, to wipe them away". Writing this book has helped me process my pain, releasing the tears of my sorrow and comprehend at a much deeper level, the compassionate heart of my Creator, whose wisdom is unfathomable and benevolence, eternal.

More importantly, I am delighted that the pain of my grief has ignited the fire that can light up the darkness of hopelessness in someone struggling to survive the irretrievable loss of a loved one, or something valuable, and find the purpose of it all, in the grand scheme of the divine artistry of creation.

Writing this book has taught me that we may never be able to recover what we lost whether that be a loved one, or a relationship, or something we cherished dearly, but when we reflect on and process our loss and make sense of it, it can produce the meaning that can help us learn life lessons we may never learn otherwise. It can teach us that, we each have the capacity to derive beauty from ashes, through intentionality and choice.

Just as emotional pain can affect the body, mind, soul and spirit; the same body, mind, soul and spirit by the power of the strength and wisdom of the Creator, can heal, restore and make existence, meaningful, inspiring a hope, that can transcend the limitations of this life.

May I take this opportunity to thank each one of you, for taking the time to read this, to understand that grief of any loss, unaddressed can potentially lead to mental ill-health and consequently, to mental illness which has a ripple effect on all those around us. In order to do well, we have got to be well, in other words our 'well-being' determines our 'well-doing'.

www.ingramcontent.com/pod-product-compliance
Lightning Source LLC
LaVergne TN
LVHW022305200926
848481LV00004B/1226
9798905102530